This Journal belongs to

....

Created by Wisdom Truth Ministries in conjunction with Ministers Desk.
For more resources, please visit WisdomTruthMinistries.com

Made in the USA
Las Vegas, NV
02 September 2021

29475103R00072